OF GRACE'S RESOUNDING CAWS

(AND FIVE POEMS ABOUT HONEY)

LAEL EWY

KNOTTED ROAD PRESS

Of Grace's Resounding Caws
(And Five Poems About Honey)
Copyright © 2018 Lael Ewy
All rights reserved

Published 2018 by Knotted Road Press
www.KnottedRoadPress.com

ISBN: 978-1-64470-010-5

Cover art:
ID 155324206 © arroyo | iStockPhoto.com
ID 5285364 © Loveliestdreams | Dreamstime.com

Cover and Interior design copyright © 2018
Knotted Road Press
www.KnottedRoadPress.com

This book is licensed for your personal enjoyment only. All rights reserved. This is a work of fiction. All characters and events portrayed in this book are fictional, and any resemblance to real people or incidents is purely coincidental. This book, or parts thereof, may not be reproduced in any form without permission.

#1

Touch a match to honey
and you'll get what happens
when love happens: the brief
sizzle and the lingering
smoke, the acrid
sacrifice to a bland
and distended heaven.

2 MARCH

Finally the sun
bare, bright, the falling collars.
Tomorrow's birthday
portends future empty shelves.
A sunbeam darkens: crow's shade.

WENDELL BECOMES AWARE OF SEXUAL TENSION

Before the age of twenty,

                                        or so,

all sex is personal:

                                          angst rides

like tight jeans scraping

                                          a hip

or belly. With the body

                                          awash

in its own torments,

                                          most miss,

early, the pheromones

                                                   of others,

signals—a flash of eye,

                                                       a turn

of thigh, the subtle play

                                                      of a lip

from across the room,

                                                     a voice

pitched just above

                                                  the state

of day. These he sees now,

                                                         loud

as the meaning a word shapes

                                                   on first

reading.

TWO APHORISMS

1. She seemed to understand doors implicitly, but then how else would a cat understand a door?

2. It would be nice to believe in animism, that that crow could be your mother, that moth flitting in the dim light the words she said to you.

HONEY

Sticky is
the price of sweet
the gloss of sweat
the glide
of the lips'

                                                                                         beckoning

back to
the breeding

                                                                                          suckle

and the earth's
flat slap

                                                                                        meeting

our soft
stumbles.

WHAT THE DEVIL SEES WHEN HE LOOKS IN THE MIRROR

The goatee that always needs a trim (a dapper devil
    is a massive undertaking!)
The eyelines of laughing through anguish eternal:
    quotation marks around statements ensouled
Skin the color of burlwood, the patina of constant
    struggle
A puff of sulphur, a pall of myrrh
Cheekbones tangentially related to everything
An image in obverse: the shadow of you.

VESTIGES OF HOW IT WENT TOGETHER

An engraved arrow with a hole next to,
the subtle steel of the head of a screw--
tenebrous tubes and shadows of flash,
a long, blond curl shaven off
the inside, a sign it's gone too far.

WORSHIP (AGAIN, AS THE HEATHEN DO)

The moon moderates
mood, so hail a bright
sigh to our Mother,
the sky, our teacher,
our laurel,
our gloom.

#3 (THE PART ABOUT THE DANCING DEAD)

Our drunken lot
it was to meet
imagined souls
and dance the ghost
waltz atop our augurs,
straddled across
dour miracle stones:
what were we fencing
in? The graves
which stood laughing
still; in the corner of the lot
a lone bee patrols.

WE SING

We sing very well, we Mennonites;
we sing at the drop of a leaf, like God's
very larks. But do we listen? Do we hear
the sounds of our voices, echoing back,
the grumble of traffic, the crows cawing,
the sirens wailing, blended in?

THE VENERATION OF THE LAMB

The children no longer thump
along the wood floor, no
longer make the sanctuary
resound with their joy
of liberation when "children's
time" comes up. Perhaps

they have none left, or are just
so clubbed empty by God
that there's no difference
between the outside and the in

.

UNTITLED

I'm heartsick at that ash
tree and at the little boy beyond it.
He plays with his ball in the street.

And it's not because he will die
or the tree will die of that I will
die that I am heartsick,

but that the tree is there, and the little boy,
and that I am there with them.

A HONEY POEM (#4, MORNING TRAFFIC)

Downtown is glacial--
paced like cold
oil and as thick as think:
in the cars, people finish
texts, stuff their maws
or just stare off, polishing
up the night's ends
before work and all its suds
scour time, joy, the grip,
and the cling of all lost chances
to swallow honey.

HEARING "THE LARK ASCENDING," LIGHT RAIN,

Modern architecture, the contentment
of joy passing over,
the collusion of damp,
rectilinear forms, concrete,
beige-stippled with coarse rock,
and here, o my soul,
the tiny imprint
of a fossil shell.

AFFIRMATION

Just above the wan smile
a flattened eye, the squinch
leading to lines late in life,
the penance for pursed lips,
a little lie that swells avoidance;
"I'd like to affirm that," she says,
and our contentions dismissed,
fall, blown petals of mum.

TRUTH TOLD

he had hundreds, woodcock and ramspring,

                                      hardened

words of putty and fill—his workshop flameth over.
    Grandpa's

                             saddle lay crushing;

the '70s were hard on horses. A knotted oak became

                                  Modernism

on three legs, catalpa Frank Lloyd Wright on a
    half-shell.

                                   Unbidden

we partook of the death of an aura. Awls scratched
    the names

of dead horses.

THE TOOL

Wrenches and ratchets and sockets and drivers of
    screws,
dead-

                      blow hammers , the honest

detritus and many wrecked Englishes, thumped,
pounded and screwed

                into place, the stretch and strain of steel

on steel grinds against the fragile flesh, the force of
    muscle

                              multiplied.

JUST THIS

Even our sins are tired, glowing
out from drooping, thoracic stoves,
implying transgressions,
a sternum beyond reaching.
But when found, the same old fumbling
with buckles and zips, the straps of bras,
the feigned delight at dumpy tits,
soft cocks only half alive. It was

a way to add spice to the tale, knowing
the narration had never
been leavened, un-kneaded; our
yeasty agitations giving
heat confounded with motion,
the crust of making what
we should have squeezed with tingling
fingers through the gut-fever
of our most solid intuitions.

GRACE

You can almost see the flicker—
A few leaves remain on the locusts
lining the front yard's west.
This leaf, that one: it's accidental;
the pile of last summer's bounty
lies in the gutter now, dropped,
a shade since it shimmered last
fall, a proud red. The fading lump
rots, lets out an earthy funk
awaiting the freezing rain.

IF ONLY

The locust's ferny branches

                                                     reach

for a sullen sky. Burned, now,
and decomposing, its ambitions

                                                     creep

toward a sappy soil. Inside,
bacteria glom into colonies,

                                                   pitch

out chemical signals; a vast
intelligence rights us.

IN THE GARDEN

To speed a pleasure
to its end is to work
in purpose to the next
pleasure, to deny
the tense--this velvet
feeling, this melting
butter, this yielding
of fur, this close
encompassing
pressure--as the world
centers,
terrified,
on us.

IN EDEN

it was always spring,

                                      the right time

for cruelty, we are told.

                                      Between the tree

of life, a spring,

                                    set for the woodcocks

whose flesh

                had just now settled on their bones. Eve felt

a quickening--

    an angel, all tail and whispering through its feathers

her fate, the way of God

                                        trod the matter

of all flesh.

A POEM ABOUT HONEY (#5)

Honey drops
from the mouth
of the demiurge--
or at least from the sweet neck
of the clerk at Old Navy, all base
and all rouge, all spike-
haired and frosted
bangs, lips
the coral of imps'
dreams, eyes
as empty as "O"

AMPHIBIAN

Between the two airs,
the difference is light:
the way a cobweb moves
when dew drops off it--
slight, yet possible.

ABOUT THE AUTHOR

Lael Ewy's work has appeared in *Denver Quarterly*, *New Orleans Review*, and an anthology, *Troubles Swapped for Something Fresh*. He does satire in *EastWesterly Review*, an online journal at www.postmodernvillage.com and the OnWords commentary on KMUW, Wichita's NPR affiliate.

Lael has taught composition and literature since 1999, most recently as a Lecturer in English at Wichita State University. He has also trained peer support workers in the mental health field.

ABOUT KNOTTED ROAD PRESS

Knotted Road Press fiction specializes in dynamic writing set in mysterious, exotic locations.

Knotted Road Press non-fiction publishes autobiographies, business books, cookbooks, and how-to books with unique voices.

Knotted Road Press creates DRM-free ebooks as well as high-quality print books for readers around the world.

With authors in a variety of genres including literary, poetry, mystery, fantasy, and science fiction, Knotted Road Press has something for everyone.

Knotted Road Press
www.KnottedRoadPress.com

www.ingramcontent.com/pod-product-compliance
Lightning Source LLC
Chambersburg PA
CBHW071223070526
44584CB00019B/3137